Hello!
I am a Whale.

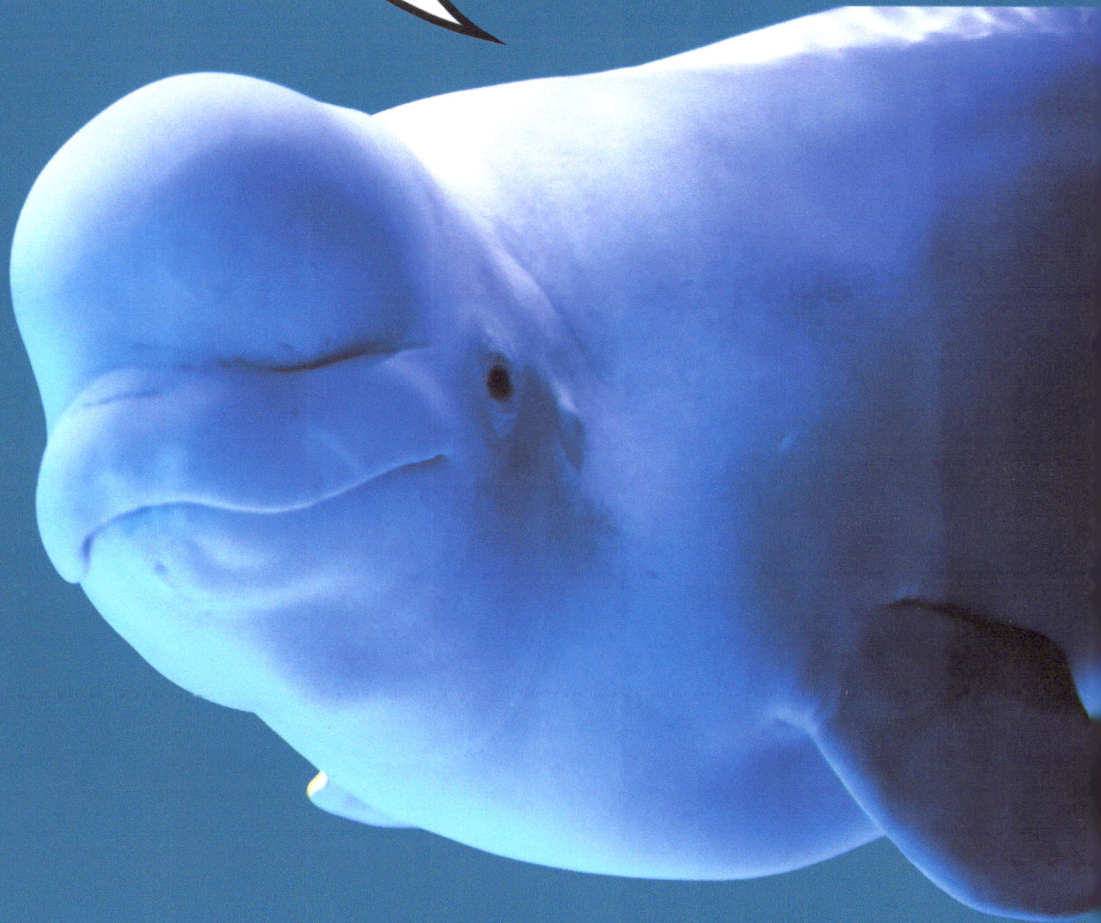

I0115155

Whales are mammals just like humans.

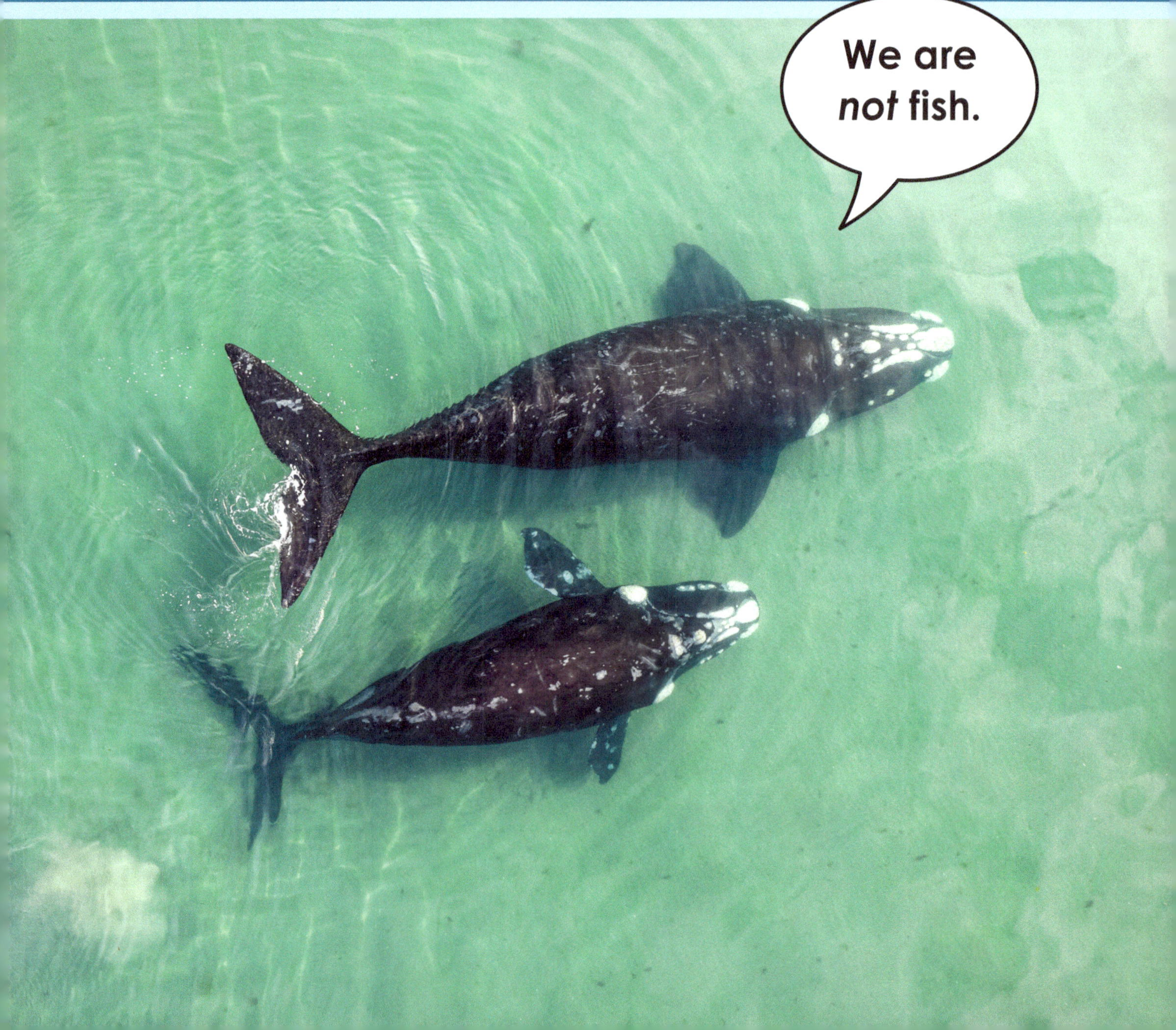
We are *not* fish.

I have a lot in common with YOU!

Whales are born, breathe air, and nurse their young with milk.

Whales can live in both warm and cold water.

Whales are found in oceans all around the world!

Some whales dive really deep to find food or avoid predators.

I can dive deeper than most submarines.

Some whale species travel long distances during migration.

We are world travelers.

Whales travel from cold areas to warm ones to meet other whales.

Whales use the Earth's magnetic field
to find their way across oceans.

Many whales use "echolocation". That means they send sounds out and the sounds bounce back.

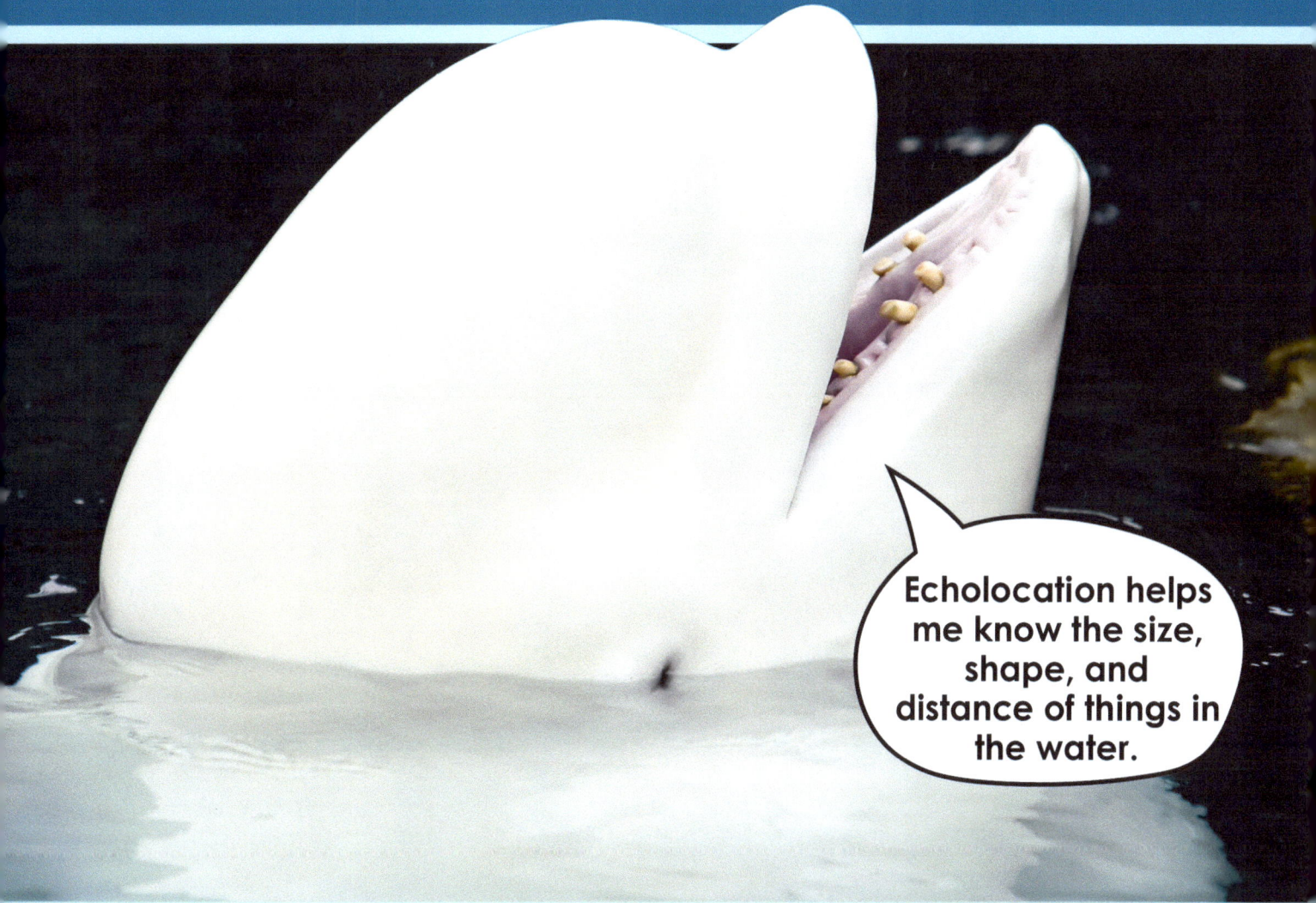

Echolocation helps me know the size, shape, and distance of things in the water.

When the sound bounces back, it shows the whale where something is located.

Whales use their tails or "flukes" to propel themselves through the water.

I am a very graceful swimmer.

Some whales are famous for their great leaps out of the water. It's called "breaching".

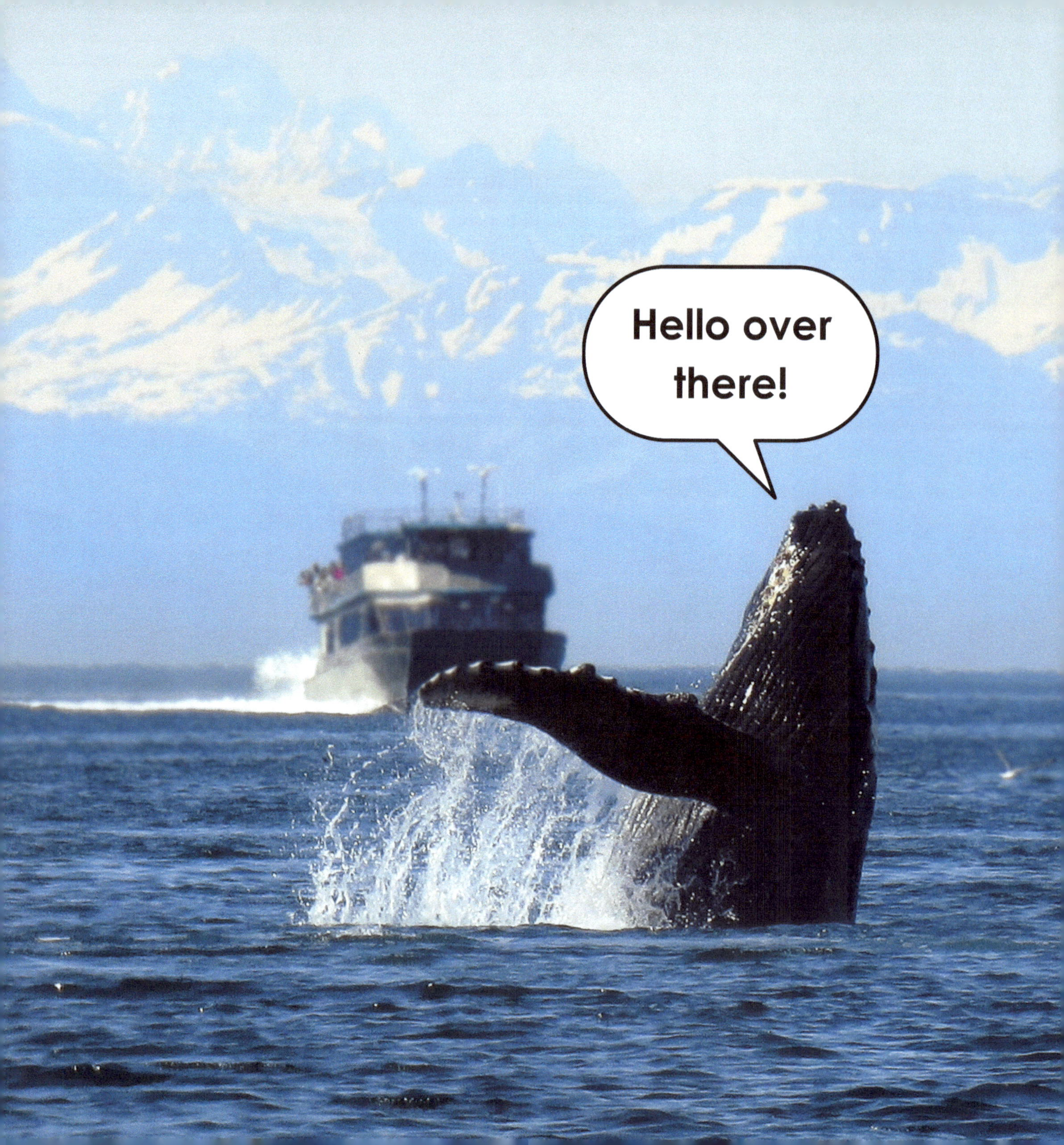
Hello over there!

Whales use breaching to communicate, play, to know their location, and to clean themselves.

The blue whale is the largest animal on Earth.

I am even bigger than the largest dinosaurs.

A baby whale can weigh as much as a small car when it's born.

Some species, like the sperm whale, have the largest brains on Earth.

My big brain makes me a very smart and social animal.

Whales use sounds like clicks, whistles, and songs that can be heard from far away.

I'm known for having the most special and beautiful songs that can last hours.

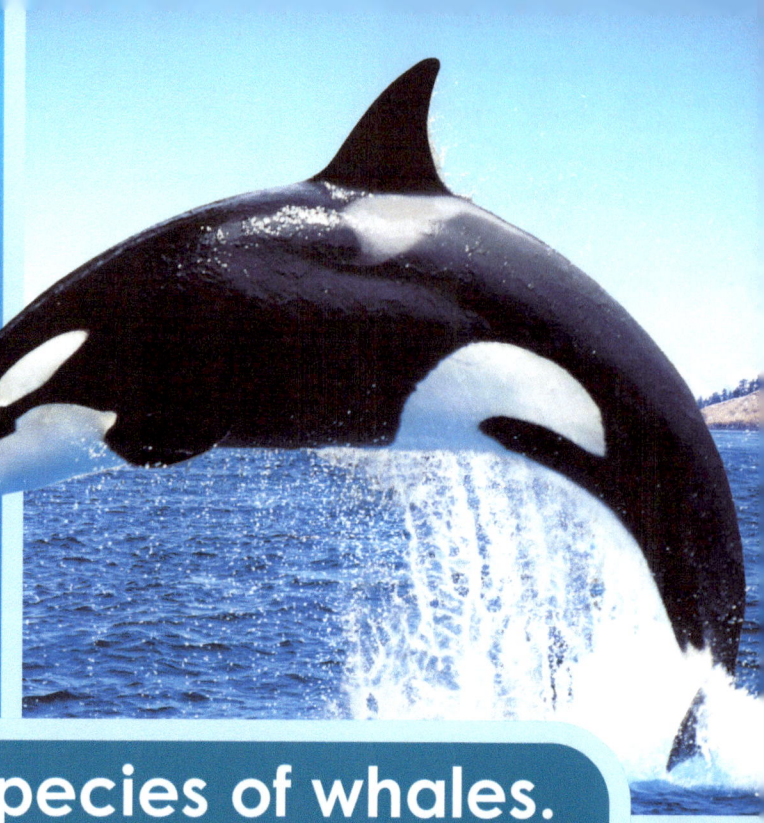

There are about 90 species of whales.
Each with it's own special look.

The skin of some whales, like the humpback, can be covered in barnacles.

Baby whales are called "calves". They are born tail-first so they don't drown.

Calves are born in the water, and mothers help them to the surface for their first breath.

Different whales have different diets.

Some whales eat tiny organisms in the water, fish or seals.

Orcas also known as "killer whales", are the main predators of other whales.

Whales often travel in groups called "pods".

Our pod works together hunting, protection and even playing.

Pods usually have 5 to 30 whales, but some have been seen up to 100.

Whales don't sleep like humans. They rest one half of their brain at a time.

Keeping one side of my brain awake lets me breath while resting.

The sperm whale, sleep vertically, with their heads down and tails up!

It's like sleeping in a headstand.

Whales can live over 100 years.

Want more?

Hello parents!

scan here

Visit us to find out about new releases and ***FREE*** offers. We'll let you know when we have a new release coming out and how you can get it for FREE.

And you can cast your vote for what book we make next!

or visit here

ActiveBrainsBooks.com

---

scan here

Let us know what you think. As an independent publisher, your honest reviews mean a lot to us and our business. We'd love to hear from you!

or visit here

amazon.com/review/create-review/

FOLLOW US on Amazon.

amazon.com/author/activebrainsbooks

ActiveBrainsBooks.com

ACTIVE BRAINS

www.ingramcontent.com/pod-product-compliance
Lightning Source LLC
Chambersburg PA
CBHW060845270326
41933CB00003B/196